How to Respond

The Lodge

Revised Edition

L. James Rongstad

CPH

SAINT LOUIS

This series was initiated to meet a need expressed by the members of The Lutheran Church—Missouri Synod in convention in 1975. The books were developed first under the umbrella of the Synod's Board for Evangelism, now part of the Board for Congregational Services.

Originally published as *How to Respond to The Lodge* in The Response Series, © 1977 Concordia Publishing House.

Copyright © 1977, 1995 Concordia Publishing House
3558 S. Jefferson Avenue, St. Louis, MO 63118-3968
Manufactured in the United States of America

Revised edition 1995

Library of Congress Cataloging-in-Publication Data

Rongstad, L. James.
    The Lodge / L. James Rongstad.—Rev. ed.
       p.   cm.   —(How to respond series)
    Rev. ed. of: How to respond to ... the Lodge. © 1977.
    Includes bibliographical references.
    ISBN 0-570-04670-X
    1. Freemasons. 2. Freemasonry—Religious aspects—Lutheran Church. I. Rongstad, L. James. How to respond to—the Lodge. II. Title. III. Series.
HS395.R67   1995
366.9'1—dc20   95-23063

2 3 4 5 6 7 8 9 10 11   06 05 04 03 02 01 00 99 98 97

The Author

Rev. L. James Rongstad, a native of Minnesota, now resides in Louisiana. Following high school, the author spent five years in the United States Navy before entering Concordia Theological Seminary, Springfield, IL, from which he graduated in 1963. His first congregation was in Selma, AL.

Rev. Rongstad's interest in the spiritual implications of membership in a religious lodge grew out of his concern that Christians maintain an undivided witness to the one and only Gospel of Jesus Christ. The author clearly shows the incompatibility between religious universalism as exemplified in the lodges and the explicit Christian confession and testimony called for by the Savior: "Whoever acknowledges Me before men, I will also acknowledge him before My Father in heaven. But whoever disowns Me before men, I will disown him before My Father in heaven" (Matthew 10:32–33).

Contents

Introduction

While the purpose of this book is to help you speak to the problems that the lodge creates for biblical Christianity, we would be remiss if we were to ignore the lodge's many positive aspects. In some ways, the lodge and its members remind us that we could do more in serving our neighbor.

Fraternalism

Americans are joiners. No matter what interests a person may have, someone, somewhere, has organized the right organization for him or her. Americans want to associate with other people and be a part of movements. The lodge provides a close-knit group of people with similar backgrounds and interests. True concern for each other is often expressed in a variety of ways, such as defending each other and caring for families and aging fellow members. Knowing that other lodge members will come to your support is a great incentive to maintain a good standing.

Loyalty

Seldom, if ever do you hear lodge members bad mouth their organization, their leaders, or their fellow members. They really stick together. Any differences they may have are handled discreetly. We Christians could learn much here. Often, it seems, we not only find reason to "knock" our pastor or fellow members, but we do it openly, too, in the public press. We need to watch our tongues, not bear false witness against our neighbor, and always speak the truth in love.

Patriotism

Even though it is now a generation in the past, the war in Vietnam has had a serious negative effect on patriotism. The politically correct attitude continually finds fault with American policies. However, this is still the world's greatest free country. Pride in our heritage must be increased. If not, it will decrease, and with it our determination to keep our freedoms in effect. We admire lodges for their patriotic emphasis.

Moral Teachings

With the sinking of public morality, we can only praise the lodge for teaching and inculcating moral values in harmony with the Ten Commandments. We commend the lodge's stress on the importance of a virtuous life.

Humanitarianism

The lodge spends a great deal of energy, time, and money to support hospitals and homes for the aged. Much time and effort are devoted to circuses, post-season football games, and the like in order to raise funds for charitable causes. These are magnificent gestures of human compassion. We thank God for these works and acts of charity. Over the years, many Christians have been helped and healed by these charitable endeavors. We Christians, again, could be doing much more in comparison.

If the lodge were to confine itself to these matters, Christians would have no quarrel. The lodge, however, has made and continues to stress the importance of religion in its organization—and has official doctrines about the core issues of Scripture and the whole Christian church. As a religion, it must be evaluated on the basis of all that God has revealed to us about our faith and life.

The Challenge to Christianity

Sören Kierkegaard said, "Christendom has done away with Christianity without being quite aware of it." Many 20th-century Christians are, and have been, giving away their heritage to the modern philosophy of liberalism with its distorted ideas of tolerance and compromise. Moral values, the basis for establishing life-styles, are being determined by public opinion rather than God's Word. Our declining self-discipline and our rising self-indulgence can be compared to sinking ground and shifting sand. The Holy Bible, the only sure and reliable foundation for moral and ethical values, is being undermined. Scriptural authority is now called into question. What was once clearly identified as the "Voice of God," the Holy Scriptures are often considered merely the opinions of those who wrote them. The Bible, for many Americans, is just another good book.

While not a new organization, the Masonic Lodge clearly promotes a philosophy of theological liberalism. Its goals demonstrate distorted ideas of tolerance and compromise that ignore the clear truth of God's Word. "The goals of Masonry are to unite the world under the umbrella of Masonic doctrine that teaches the fatherhood of God, the brotherhood of man, and the immortality of the soul. Masons foresee the day when all religious division and sectarianism ... will be wiped away, and a new era of universal peace, brotherhood, and religious faith will emerge" (*The Secret Teachings of the Masonic Lodge,* p. 32). Such goals certainly do not stand firm on the truth of God as revealed in Jesus Christ.

The time has come to stand up to the rush into manmade religious theories. Change must come! We need to return to the Holy Bible as the authoritative Word of God. This volume is written in order to preserve among us our priceless heritage of a people saved by God's grace through faith in Jesus Christ, the Savior of the world. May you be ready to give an answer to the lodge.

1

History and Organization of the Lodge

As an organization, Freemasonry began in A.D. 1717. Two clergymen, Dr. James Anderson, a Presbyterian, and Dr. John Theophilus Desaguliers, a French Huguenot turned Anglican, stimulated others to form a select group. This inspired four London speculative lodges to come together to form the first Grand Lodge.

Negro Freemasonry started in the United States on March 6, 1775, in Boston, when the degrees of Masonry were conferred upon Prince Hall and 14 other Black men in a military lodge (No. 441 on the Irish Register) in the English Army attached to the 38th Regiment. It is alleged that Prince Hall was born in Barbados, British West Indies, that he came to Boston and became leader of "free" Negroes of that city, and was ordained a minister.

> **When and where did Masonry begin? What were the first Masons like? ... [T]he average Masonic book today which deals with such issues is based on pure speculation and an overactive imagination. (Robert Morey, *The Truth about Masons*, p. 9)**

On September 9, 1784, the Grand Lodge of England issued a charter for African Lodge No. 459 of Boston. It was instrumental in forming the first Negro Grand Lodge in the United States.

These historical facts, however, do not stop the

Ancient, Free, and Accepted Masons from teaching prospective members that their origin is thousands of years old. For example, Masonic teaching states that Hiram, king of Tyre, aided in the building of the Jerusalem temple at the time of Solomon. He supplied trees, carpenters, and masons for this project and had close relations with King Solomon concerning problems of mutual interest. *New Age,* the official organ of the Supreme Council Southern Jurisdiction, claims this relationship "tends to confirm the belief that there was some close Masonic tie between them" (April 1961, p. 30). The Bible (1 Kings 5) does report that Hiram provided materials to Solomon for the building of the temple, but that the two rulers had a "Masonic tie" à la today is beyond any credibility.

The Holy Bible—Masonic Edition, published by John A. Hertel Co., claims of the antiquity of the lodge, "It is admitted that Masonry is descended from the ancient mysteries. These were first arranged when the constellation Leo was at the summer solstice. Thus the antiquity of Masonry was written in the starry heavens" (Revised Edition, 1957, p. 21).

Albert Pike, in *Morals and Dogma,* says, "The first Masonic Legislator whose memory is preserved to us by history, was Buddha, who, about a thousand years before the Christian era, reformed the religion of Manous. He called to the Priesthood all men, without distinction of caste, who felt themselves inspired by God to instruct men" (p. 277).

> Masonry, with its teachings, rituals, customs and practices, and secrecy, has had an impact on its auxiliary organizations such as the Eastern Star and Job's Daughters as well as other lodge organizations such as the Moose, Eagles, Elks, and National Grange.

On May 17, 1963, the *Birmingham News* (Alabama), in a special edition dedicated to the Masonic Order, reprinted a statement made by T. G. Brabston, the late distinguished leader of the Southeastern Shrine Association: "The origin of Freemasonry is lost in the nebulous mist of unrecorded history. It has been identified with the building of King Solomon's temple. The reliable history of Masonry covers the past 250 years."

Whatever the true facts, the lodge continues to rewrite history. Some would have us believe that the use of the word *lodge* in A.D. 1278 to refer to a hut or shed for shelter at a construction site was really a "lodge" in the sense of an organization like we have today. Such temporary buildings housed tools and served as workshops, offices, and sleeping quarters for the workmen, some of whom were stone masons, while they were away from their homes. These ancient "lodges" would compare today with the oil rigs in the Gulf of Mexico that serve as temporary homes for the men at work.

Occasionally a Mason may be heard to claim that great men of the past have been fellow Masons—men such as John the Baptizer, the evangelist John, and Noah. These particular claims are, at best, the fruits of fertile imaginations and pride in the order. However, it is true that a number of famous American men have been Masons. Hertel's *The Holy Bible—Masonic Edition* claims 15 presidents have been Masons: Washington, Jefferson, Madison, Monroe, Jackson, Polk, Buchanan, Johnson, Garfield, McKinley, T. Roosevelt, Taft, Harding, F. D. Roosevelt, and Truman. Some think Pierce and Taylor were also in the number. Furthermore, it is claimed that Lincoln and Grant had proposed to become Masons, but death came to both before they took the vows. In addition, many U.S. senators and congressmen have been and are Masons. The American name most cherished by Masons is that of George Washington.

In the absence of documentary evidence to link Freemasonry to any time prior to A.D. 1717, those who claim ancient origins for the Masonic Lodge simply ignore the facts. The more reliable, honest, and respected Masonic leaders of today freely admit the truth and are not anxious to support a lengthy history.

The Term *Freemason*

The term *Freemason,* according to Masonic sources, predates the organizational origins of the lodge. A number of explanations are suggested. (1) Masons worked in free stone, which could be carved, and hence were called "free-stone masons," later shortened to "freemasons." (2) They were free men, not serfs. (3) They were free to move from place to place as they might desire. (4) They were given the freedom of the towns or localities in which they worked. (5) They were free of the rules and regulations that were usually imposed on members of guilds.

These "freemasons" are referred to as being "operative," because they worked at their specific trades— builders, stone masons, and architects engaged in construction work. Because they usually worked closely together and because they frequently were away from home, they formed a tight-knit group in which they shared discussions on philosophies, politics, religion, and all other interests of their society. Gradually these "operatives" were joined by others who were not of their crafts, but because they were interested in the background and teachings of the operative fraternity, they were considered to be "accepted" masons. Eventually the "accepted" masons outnumbered the "operatives" and took control of the "speculative" symbols and secrets of the lodge. Now all members are accepted as "speculative masons." Hence the name "Ancient, Free, and *Accepted* Masons."

Historic Influences on Christianity

Even as Masons have influenced American politics

and history, so also has Masonry influenced American religious life. In 1769 the first Knights Templar degrees were conferred by the lodge. This group of Christians was assumed into Freemasonry and made a part of the York Rite in order to make the lodge more acceptable to professing Christians. The Knights Templar are inspired by the Crusaders of medieval times and are supposed to be militant supporters of Christianity. Some members think that the Knights Templar, also called the "Christian Degree," is not objectionable and even point with pride to their Order. They tend to forget, however, that by their association with this degree, they also support the teachings of the whole lodge.

In its beginnings, the lodge had a Christian orientation and today still makes frequent reference to the Bible. But as it evolved, the lodge developed the concept of Deism: a generalized, nonspecific belief about who God is. This subtle shift of emphasis, done with great piety, has blinded many Christians to the truth about the Triune God. This "Supreme Architect of the Universe" is not the God revealed in Scripture!

In 1913, the Masonic Grand Master in England, the Duke of Sussex, gave rise to universalism in the lodge when he influenced the English lodge to omit Christ's name from its prayers. This influence of universalism has carried over to the practice of omitting the name of Jesus in all its public prayers, which has become the "nondenominational" way to pray.

An additional indication of Masonry's influence on American religious life is seen in the fact that many church buildings of various denominations have cornerstones displaying the lodge symbols. Furthermore, most lodge organizations are active in conducting funerals. Lodges are serious about practicing their theology of universalism. The ritual and practice of the lodge have become its own religion.

Lodge Organization and Structure

Freemasonry in the United States consists of the three basic degrees of the Blue Lodge: Entered Apprentice, Fellow Craft, and Master Mason.

The expression "Blue Lodge" is usually explained by one of two theories. One is that "operative masons" (medieval craft workers) considered the blue sky to be symbolic of the purity of God, which in turn reminded them to work harder to keep pure their own lives. The other theory is that shortly after "speculative Masonry" (symbolic Masonry, begun in 1717) came into existence, the color blue was substituted for white as the official color for the first Grand Lodge of England. This was done presumably because blue was the color of the Order of the Garter, of which a number of Masonic leaders were members.

It appears that most lodges, especially the Masonic Lodge, practice racial discrimination. Within the last 20 years such bias has officially been removed from the constitutions of most lodge organizations. However, Masons freely admit that the casting of one black ball in a vote can avoid the "unanimous consent" necessary for any candidate to be "entered" into the lodge.

Beyond the Blue Lodge, the Master Mason may choose one of two paths to follow (or neither): the Scottish Rite, which has 30 degrees, and the American Rite (sometimes called the York Rite), which has 10 degrees. The first three degrees of the Blue Lodge are the only essential degrees through which all Masons must pass. All other degrees are optional.

The York Rite

The York Rite, or American Rite Masonry, has 10 degrees beyond the Blue Lodge, divided into three categories. Degrees 4–7 comprise the "Chapter." They are the "Capitular Degrees." In numerical order, they are called

Mark Master, Past Master, Most Excellent Master, and Royal Arch Mason. The second grouping, called the "Council," is comprised of degrees 8–10. These are called Royal Master, Select Master, and Super Excellent Master. The third grouping is called the "Commandery" and is comprised of the Order of Red Cross, Order of Knights of Malta, and finally Order of Knights Templar, the highest degree.

The Scottish Rite

The degree structure of Scottish Rite Masonry is built around four groupings. The Lodge of Perfection has 11 degrees (4–14), commonly called the "Ineffable Degrees." The Council of Princes of Jerusalem has two degrees (15–16), called the "Historical Grades." The Chapter of Rose Croix has two degrees (17–18), called the "Philosophical Grades." The Consistory has the last 14 degrees (19–32), called the "Traditional and Chivalric Grades." The Thirty-Third (33rd) Degree is the "Official Grade" and is strictly honorary. Having earned the 32nd degree, the

> All Shriners are Masons, but not all Masons are Shriners.

Mason who wants to become "elite" and has the money and honor necessary to be admitted can become a Shriner, a side order of Masonry.

Side Orders of Masonry

The Ancient Arabic Order of the Nobles of the Mystic Shrine are the most visible of all side orders of Masonry. Members of the Shrine, thus Shriners, are very visible in parades, wearing their uniforms topped by the fez (head covering with a tassel) and usually riding some kind of vehicle—a funny car, a motorcycle, etc. Shriners are heavily involved in charitable activities. They operate hospitals, emphasizing the care and treatment of burn victims, thus creating a favorable image of Shriners in particular and Masons in general.

Other side orders of Masonry are the Tall Cedars in Lebanon of the United States of America, Knights of the Red Cross of Constantine, and Acacia Fraternity. Affiliated female organizations include the Order of the Eastern Star, White Shrine of Jerusalem, Order of Amaranth, Daughters of the Nile, and Daughters of Mokanna. Youth Organizations are Order of the Builders, Order of Demolay, Order of Job's Daughters, and Order of the Rainbow.

Authority in the Lodge

The lodge, whether local or state Grand Lodge, is not democratically governed. Rather, rule is autocratic. The Worshipful Master of a local lodge, for example, has supreme and total control. The bylaws of the local lodge do set minimum standards of conduct but usually are so worded as to place all authority in the hands of the elected leader.

2

The Lodge as a Religion

What is religion? When does a group become a religion? What does it take to be religious?

A dictionary defines religion as that which (1) expresses the service and adoration of God—or a god—in forms of worship; (2) has a system of faith and worship; (3) professes and practices religious beliefs, collective religious observances, or rites; (4) demonstrates a devotion of fidelity; or (5) expresses the awareness and conviction of the existence of a supreme being thereby arousing reverence, love, gratitude, and the will to obey and serve. Does the Masonic Lodge fit the definition?

Teachings about God

The first question asked of the candidate for lodge membership as he enters the Entered Apprentice Degree, the first step of the three-step "Blue Lodge," is if he believes in God. If he says no, he is disqualified from membership. However, the lodge does not

> Every Masonic Lodge is a temple of religion; and its teachings are instruction in religion. For here are inculcated ... Faith, Hope, and Charity. Here we meet as brethren, to learn to know and love each other. ... This is the true religion revealed to the ancient patriarchs; which Masonry has taught for many centuries, and which it will continue to teach as long as time endures. (Pike, *Morals and Dogma*, p. 213)

want the candidate to identify who he considers God to be, because the lodge has its own identification of God as the "Supreme Architect of the Universe," or the "Supreme Grand Master," or the "Nameless One of a Hundred Names." In other words, Masonry doesn't care what the individual lodge member believes about God as long as the member admits to some belief in a supreme being. Carl Claudy, a noted Masonic author writes, "A belief in God is essential to a Mason, but ... any god will do, so [long as] he is your God" (*Little Masonic Library,* 4:32, quoted in *Secret Teachings,* p. 111).

Teachings about Eternal Reward

Masonic teachings promise eternal life as a reward for a moral life in this world. As the Entered Apprentice is presented for membership in the lodge, he is given a lambskin apron and is told:

> The Lamb has in all ages been deemed an emblem of innocence. By the lambskin, therefore, the Mason is reminded of that purity of life and conduct which is essential to his gaining admission to the Celestial Lodge above, where the Supreme Architect of the Universe presides. (*Louisiana Masonic Monitor,* pp. 44–45)

This creed of the lodge says simply, Be good and you'll go to heaven. Live a morally upright life, and God, whoever He is, will receive you on the other side.

The Christian believes otherwise. "Now this is eternal life: that they may know You, the only true God, and Jesus Christ, whom You have sent" (John 17:3). Jesus was and is the most controversial figure in all history. Why? Because there is no salvation without Him. He is the center of the Christian faith.

Jesus makes Himself the center of controversy when

He narrows salvation to Himself only as true God, the Word made flesh. He died on the cross to pay for the sins of the whole world. He was and is the innocent Lamb, the only Savior from sin. No amount of pious, moral living will earn eternal life. Eternal life is the free gift of God's grace. It cannot be earned nor given as an award for righteous living. "If Masonry teaches a man's good works can fit him for heaven, this makes believing on Jesus as personal Savior merely optional" (*Secret Teachings,* pp. 80–81). The Masonic Lodge has created its own theology and belief system separate and apart from that of Christianity.

> Just as Moses lifted up the snake in the desert, so the Son of Man must be lifted up, that everyone who believes in Him may have eternal life. ... Whoever believes in Him is not condemned, but whoever does not believe stands condemned already because he has not believed in the name of God's one and only Son. (John 3:14–15, 18)

Teachings about Moral Living

Every Masonic lodge contains three indispensable pieces of furniture that are referred to as the "three great lights of Masonry." They are the Square, the Compass, and the Sacred Book. The Square is what a carpenter uses to measure right angles and to mark wood in order to cut a perfect line to match an adjoining piece of wood. The Compass is an instrument used by draftsmen and builders to inscribe a circle. Together Square and Compass symbolize the necessity of a Mason keeping his life "in square" and circumscribed in his relationships with others, especially with brother Masons.

The Sacred Book is that volume recognized as being holy. It can be the Bible, the Torah, the Qur'an, or any other such book. In an effort to be all inclusive and to offend no one's religious background, Freemasonry sees itself as above partisan religious beliefs. Albert Pike says, "The Bible is an indispensable part of the furniture of a *Christian* Lodge, only because it is the sacred book of the Christian religion. The Hebrew Pentateuch in a Hebrew Lodge, and Koran in a Mohammedan one, belong on the Altar. ... We have no other concern with your religious creed" (*Morals and Dogma,* p. 11). This attitude of condescension toward specific religions is really an elevation of the lodge as a super-religion.

Another symbol that helps define the Masonic theology is the Ashlar. Ashlar is stone as it is taken from the quarry. Rough and jagged, it is to remind the Mason of his imperfect nature. The gavel reminds him that as it chips away by pounding the rough and jagged edges of the ashlar, so he also is to remove the imperfections of his personality and life-style.

All of these symbols express Masonic teaching regarding the nature of people. Masonry teaches that humanity is not originally sinful, just imperfect. If a person works faithfully at keeping the principles and teachings of the lodge, then he will be ushered into the "Grand Lodge Above," where the "Supreme Architect of the Universe" presides. This is the religion of universalism, which denies the necessity of needing a Savior from sin. Therefore Jesus is unnecessary in the teaching of the lodge. This is why we object to lodge membership and why we have made this effort to inform and educate.

Is the Lodge a Religion?

From this author's personal experience it is nearly impossible for a lodge member to agree that it is a religion, to admit the obvious. Therefore, the following quote from a respected Masonic author should be revealing. In his *Masonic Encyclopedia* (1961), in a lengthy article on "Religion," Henry Wilson Coil says (pp. 512–13):

Some attempt to avoid the issue by saying that Freemasonry is not a religion but is religious, seeming to believe that the substitution of an adjective for a noun makes a fundamental difference. It would be as sensible to say that man had no intellect but was intellectual or that he had no honor but was honorable. ... Freemasonry certainly requires a belief in the existence of, and man's dependence upon, a Supreme Being to which he is responsible. What can a church add to that, except to bring into fellowship those who have like feelings? That is exactly what the lodge does. ...

> Jesus answered, "I am the way and the truth and the life. No one comes to the Father except through Me." (John 14:6)

It is said that Freemasonry is not sectarian, by which is meant that it has not identified itself with any well-known sect. But, if it has a religious *credo,* may it not, itself, constitute a sect to be added to the others? ... Perhaps the most we can say is that Freemasonry has not generally been regarded as a sect or denomination, though it may become so if its religious practices, creeds, tenets, and dogma increase as much in the future as they have in the past. Only by judging from external appearances and applying arbitrary gauges can we say that Freemasonry is not religion. ... Nothing herein is intended to be an argument that Freemasonry *ought* to be a religion; our purpose is simply to determine what it has *become* and *is.*

Some have claimed that lodges don't establish religion but merely recognize that God exists. Evaluate that claim in the light of the following two quotations from non-Masonic orders.

> There is no death; life is full of mysteries until
> the God of Love opens the portals of His king-
> dom and bids each passing soul a glorious wel-
> come into its eternal home. ... Let us bow our
> heads in silent prayer for our sisters who are
> waiting in the Great Auxiliary over there. (From
> the Charter Draping Ceremony, Auxiliary to the
> Fraternal Order of Eagles)

> Surely there is an after-life for all who have been
> loyal and true, a life to which light and peace
> shall come, where the burden shall be lifted and
> the heartache shall cease, where the love, the
> hope and the fulfillment that escapes us here
> shall be given to us to be ours forever. (From the
> funeral service, American Legion Auxiliary)

When lodge organizations promise their members an afterlife where the burdens of this life will be lifted and where God will welcome them to an eternal home, is this not an establishment of religion by any definition of the term?

In such religion, the uniqueness of the Christian message is lost. The Gospel, grounded in the hope of eternal life secured for us by the resurrection of Jesus from the dead, is denied by organizations that reduce salvation to mere moral living without an emphasis on sin and grace, repentance and forgiveness in Christ. The teachings of Christianity are casually lumped together with teachings of all other religions. From this mix of theology has come Masonry's "light."

Why the Secrecy if Masonry Is the Universal Religion?

The Mason who also claims to be a Christian usually

retreats into a shell of secrecy when confronted with the contradictions between the teachings of the lodge and those of Christianity. Why? Because secrecy so dominates the lodge that the candidate for membership, *before* he knows what he is getting into, must take his oath under the most severe penalties. He must promise to "always conceal and never reveal" the secrets of Masonry. He binds himself to this promise under the penalty of "having my throat cut across, my tongue torn out from its roots, and my body buried in the rough sands of the sea" (*Duncan's Masonic Ritual and Monitor,* pp. 34–35).

A contradiction exists within the lodge. It claims to have a purer truth than any of the religions, yet its "truth" is steadfastly kept secret. Should not the lodge open its closet doors and proclaim this truth openly? Albert Pike writes about the Masonic view of its so-called truth:

> Masonry teaches, and has preserved in their purity, the cardinal tenets of the old primitive faith, which underlie and are the foundation of all religions. All that ever existed have had a basis of truth; and all have overlaid that truth with errors. The primitive truths taught by the Redeemer were sooner corrupted, and intermingled and alloyed with fictions than when taught to the first of our race. Masonry is the universal morality which is suitable to the inhabitants of every clime, to the man of every creed. (*Morals and Dogma,* p. 161)

Note the Masonic condescension toward other religions—a point not evident to all its members. Having that attitude concealed may explain, in part, why even some Protestant clergymen see no problem holding membership in an organization that belittles their church's teachings. Southern Baptists, for instance, voted at their 1993 convention to allow a man's conscience be his guide—in deference most probably to the clergy who have dual memberships. Some congregations, however, see the problem. Myrtle Grove Presbyterian Church, for example, is to be commended for adopting the policy of barring Freemasons from holding a church office, heading a ministry, or teaching in church (*Morning Star*, Wilmington, NC: June 28, 1994). Further, the Church of God (Anderson, IN), on June 15, 1994, adopted a resolution by the General Assembly that said, "Freemasonry is a Christless religion that omits … the name of Jesus Christ in its prayers and rituals and has a false view of God and the nature of His salvation." In the resolution the denomination reaffirms "its historic position, which proclaims membership in secret societies and lodges which are oath bound is not compatible with the Christian loyalty to Christ."

Jesus is the light of the world (John 8:12). He also is the truth (John 14:6). There is no truth apart from Him. Pontius Pilate had trouble with that. "What is truth?" he asked (John 18:38). People of every age have had trouble with it. The lodge alone seems to rise above everyone else with its theology, claiming *its* path toward "the light" will eventually lead everyone into all the truth. Yet, that path is apart from Christ. The Christian way is to know the truth as it is revealed in Jesus. Christians need to openly share with others what we have learned of the love of God in Christ Jesus our Savior. We will play no games with the truth, nor will we hold secrets about what the truth is.

3

Salvation in the Lodge

Masonry is a Divinely appointed institution to draw men nearer to God, to give them a clearer conception of their proper relationship to God as their Heavenly Father, to men as their brethren and the ultimate destiny of the human soul. (*Iowa Quarterly Bulletin,* April 1917, p. 54)

For most of the 20th century many Masons have been willing to admit that the lodge is religious, and some would even say it is a religion. The lodge has a theology as fully developed as any recognized religion—albeit erroneous in comparison to Christianity. It is a theology that teaches very specific things about the fatherhood of God, the brotherhood of man, and the immortality of the human soul. All lodges have this theology to a greater or lesser degree, whether they are affiliated with the Masons, are one of the "animal" lodges, or are a different group using a religious ritual and philosophy.

Now that this century draws to a close and the 21st is ushered in, it is time that we not only accord the lodges religious status that they themselves claim, but that we also look deeply into what they teach. Is it compatible with Christianity? opposed to Christianity? a substitute for Christianity? a super-Christianity? You be the judge. The quotes that follow in this chapter will identify the answers we seek.

The Lodge's Theology of God

The Christian God is the Triune God, the Holy Trinity. That means that there are three persons—Father, Son, and Holy Spirit—yet one God, one Lord. An integral part of the Christian teaching about God is that God, in the person of His Son, became a human at a point in time. The Son of God was conceived by the Holy Spirit in the womb of the Virgin Mary. He was born with human flesh so that true God and true man became united in Jesus Christ. Christians also believe that the Holy Spirit proceeds from the Father and Son and creates faith in the hearts of people.

The lodges teach a different understanding of God. Albert Pike, who has been called by many fellow Masons "one of the most distinguished Masons the Western World has produced," writes,

> We do not undervalue the importance of any Truth. We utter no word that can be deemed irreverent by anyone of any faith. We do not tell the Moslem that it is only important for him to believe that there is but one God, and wholly unessential whether Mahomet was His prophet. We do not tell the Hebrew that the Messiah whom he expects was born in Bethlehem nearly two thousand years ago; and that he is a heretic because he will not so believe. And as little do we tell the sincere Christian that Jesus of Nazareth was but a man like us, or His history but the unreal revival of an older legend. To do either is beyond our jurisdiction. Masonry, of no one age, belongs to all time; of no one religion, it finds its great truths in all.
>
> To every Mason, there is a God; One, Supreme,

Infinite in Goodness, Wisdom, Foresight, Justice, and Benevolence; Creator, Disposer, and Preserver of all things. How, or by what intermediates He creates and acts, and in what way He unfolds and manifests Himself, Masonry leaves to creeds and Religions to inquire.

It [Masonry] reverences all the great reformers. It sees in Moses, the Lawgiver of the Jews, in Confucius and Zoroaster, in Jesus of Nazareth, and in the Arabian Iconoclast, Great Teachers of Morality, and Eminent Reformers, if no more: and allows every brother of the Order to assign to each such higher and even Divine Character as his Creed and Truth require. (*Morals and Dogma,* pp. 524–25)

"Great Architect of the Universe" is one of the names used publicly by Masons to identify their god. This name is a new creation of the lodge and was carefully chosen so as not to use any name for God found in the Holy Bible or any religious book. It and a few other names like the "Nameless One of a Hundred Names" are used publicly. The most secret

> **G**reat Architect of the Universe—G.A.O.T.U.: one of the primary designations for God in Masonry.

Masonic word for God, however, is never spoken out loud.

As the candidate is raised into the Master Mason Degree, he is told to assume the "five points of fellowship" (toe to toe, knee to knee, chest to chest, cheek to cheek, and mouth to ear). Then the most sacred Masonic word is whispered: *Mah—Ha—Bone.* This is God's name, he is told, and must never be spoken out loud, never revealed, and always concealed.

The Mason in the Royal Arch Degree (York Rite), a degree through which the Knight Templar is to pass on his way to the supposed "Christian Degree," has yet another secret name revealed to him at his initiation ceremony. The name of the True God, which has been "rediscovered," is *Jah—Bul—On*. "Jah" is the abbreviation for the Hebrew name of God: Jahweh or Jehovah. "Bul" or "Bal" is the name for the Assyrian god and is mentioned throughout the Old Testament as "Baal" or "Baal-peor." This was the idol God warned the Israelites to avoid at all costs, but they did not! "On" is the Egyptian sun god. This is the "trinity" for the Royal Arch Mason.

In the Knights Templar Degree, where the emphasis is supposed to be Christian, there is a strange absence of any reference to Jesus as true God and true man, divine and human. It is not mentioned that Jesus is the Savior from sin or that it is necessary for people to repent of their sin and accept the atonement of Christ as their substitute.

Once again we raise this question: Is the religion of the lodge compatible with Christianity or opposed to it?

The Lodge's Theology of Humanity

We Christians confess the scriptural truth that all people since the fall of Adam and Eve are born sinful. It is the heritage of original sin that the human race must bear, namely, to be by nature corrupt and apart from God. People are helpless to save themselves from the consequences of sin and hopeless to provide a guiltless conscience and a peaceful eternal life in heaven. "Surely I was sinful at birth, sinful from the time my mother conceived me" (Psalm 51:5). "All have sinned and fall short of the glory of God" (Romans 3:23).

Contrast that to the teachings of the lodge. "Freemasonry has taught each man can, by himself, work out his own conception of God and thereby achieve salvation" (Ward, *The Freemasonry: Its Aims and Ideals,* p. 187). Boldly Masonry claims that people are above God. They can determine who God is and on what terms they will work out their own salvation. Isn't that convenient? Humanity would then be its own god. In fact, the lodge has become its own god, lord, and savior. It is the creature dictating to the Creator. It is the lodge's piety elevated into deity.

"The fraternity is, to me, man's organized attempt in an orderly way to proceed in a direction of life that is orientated toward what he feels is creation's design for him in this universe. It is the reach of man for God" (*The Short Talk Bulletin,* Masonic Service Association of the United States, 43:5, May 1964, p. 3). Such a statement indicates that Masonry reverses the biblical teaching that it is God who reaches into people's lives, converts them, and gives them new purpose in life. St. Paul clearly expresses this truth when he writes, "But because of His great love for us, God, who is rich in mercy, made us alive with Christ even when we were dead in transgressions. ... For it is by grace you have been saved, through faith—and this not from yourselves, it is the gift of God—not by works, so that no one can boast" (Ephesians 2:4, 8–9).

> For the time will come when men will not put up with sound doctrine. Instead, to suit their own desires, they will gather around them a great number of teachers to say what their itching ears want to hear. They will turn their ears away from the truth and turn aside to myths. (2 Timothy 4:3–4)

The Lodge's Theology on Reaching Heaven

The third major teaching of the lodge is that of the immortal nature of the human soul. While that is biblical, the lodge teaches its own way to reach eternal bliss.

To achieve it [salvation] the Mason must first attain a solid conviction, founded upon reason, that he hath within him a spiritual nature, a soul that is not to die when the body is dissolved, but is to continue to exist and to advance toward perfection through all ages of eternity, and to see more and more clearly, as it draws nearer unto God, the Light of the Divine Presence. (*Morals and Dogma*, p. 855)

Here the Mason is taught that the soul continues to progress toward perfection (salvation), even *after* soul and body are separated by physical death. Both now and after the Mason dies, he must work hard, be good, and finally earn heaven—on his own. He has no need for the Savior Jesus Christ (or any savior, for that matter).

Hertel's revised Masonic edition of the Bible urges all Masons to be mindful of the symbolism of the various instruments by which man is to measure his life in order to determine his integrity for admission into "the Grand Lodge Above." Concerning the Masonic Lodge member it says, "Guided by the movable jewels of Masonry (the square, compass, level, and plumb), he builds for himself a character of unblamableness preparing himself as a successful candidate for admission in the Grand Lodge" (p. 33).

Christians have learned from the Bible that Jesus died on the cross because of His love for humanity, rose from the dead on the third day, and ascended into heaven with His glorified body. We, through faith in Jesus, will never die. On Judgment Day, our body will be raised, glorified, and rejoined to our soul. With body and soul rejoined, we will be forever in heaven. All this is a gift of God's grace to us. We have not earned it; it is a gift. St. Paul writes,

Brothers, we do not want you to be ignorant about those who fall asleep, or to grieve like the rest of men, who have no hope. We believe that Jesus died and rose again and so we believe that God will bring with Jesus those who have fallen asleep in Him. According to the Lord's own word, we tell you that we who are still alive, who are left till the coming of the Lord, will certainly not precede those who have fallen asleep. For the Lord Himself will come down from heaven, with a loud command, with the voice of the archangel and with the trumpet call of God, and the dead in Christ will rise first. After that, we who are still alive and are left will be caught up together with them in the clouds to meet the Lord in the air. And so we will be with the Lord forever. Therefore encourage each other with these words. (1 Thessalonians 4:13–18)

The *Louisiana Masonic Monitor* has the Worshipful Master reciting to the candidate for the Master Mason Degree these words: "And now, my brethren, let us see to it, and so regulate our lives by the plumb-line of justice, ever squaring our actions by the square of virtue, that when the Grand Warden of Heaven shall call for us, we may be found ready" (p. 132).

The Masonic doctrines of the immortality of the soul and works-righteousness are further illustrated in this prayer at the Masonic burial service:

Most glorious God, Author of all good and Giver of all mercy, pour down Thy blessings upon us, and strengthen our solemn engagements with the ties of sincere affection. May the present instance of mortality remind us of our own approaching fate, and, by drawing our attention toward Thee, may we be induced so to regulate our conduct here that when the moment of dissolution shall arrive at which we must quit this brief scene, we may be received into Thine everlasting kingdom, there to enjoy that uninter-

rupted and unceasing felicity which is allotted
to the souls of just men made perfect. Amen.
(*Monitor*, pp. 156–57)

The lodge teaches, along with the immortality of the
soul, a belief in the resurrection of the body. Both ideas are
seen in this statement at the burial service, which is spoken following the above-quoted prayer:

Quietly may thy body sleep in this earthly bed,
my brother. Bright and glorious be thy rising
from it. Fragrant be the acacia [evergreen] sprig
that here shall flourish. May the earliest buds of
spring unfold their beauties on this, thy body's
resting place; and here may the sweetness of the
summer's rose linger latest. Though the cold
blast of autumn may lay them in the dust, and
for a time destroy the loveliness of their existence, yet their fading is not final, and in the
springtime they shall surely bloom again. So in
the bright morning of resurrection thou shalt
spring again into newness of life. Until then,
dear brother, until then, farewell. (*Louisiana
Monitor*, p. 157)

Need we point to the glaring absence of any reference
to Jesus Christ? How obvious is the false hope that the
departed lodge member is in heaven because of the member's conduct in this life. All lodges have a committal service for the funeral of one of their members. All avoid identification with Jesus Christ but will otherwise use Christian
expressions in the prayers. A good example of theological
confusion is found in the following from the funeral ritual
of the Order of Amaranth:

Faith, as recorded by St. Paul, is the substance of
things hoped for, the evidence of things not

seen. ... It upholds us in our darkest hours, and directs the mind to the contemplation of the goodness of our Divine Father, who doeth all things well, rewarding each according to his works. ... Let us have faith in ourselves, in our associates, and struggle on against evil influences and discouragements; for by keeping Faith with one another we enhance the happiness of ourselves. Faith is the Savior and Redeemer of nations.

The Bible is held to be "the great light" of Masonry. But if this is so, why does Masonry never once warn men about hell? ... Nothing could constitute a greater disservice than to do as the Masonic Lodge does here, to make men think they will automatically go to heaven when they die because of their good works and never warn them of the penalty for rejecting God's true salvation." (*Secret Teachings,* pp. 153–54)

"*Faith* is the Savior and Redeemer of nations"? The Christian faith has never taught that this is so. Rather, Jesus Christ is the "Savior and Redeemer of nations" and the hope of eternal life in heaven. This is clearly stated by St. Paul:

> But when the kindness and love of God our Savior appeared, He saved us, not because of righteous things we had done, but because of His mercy. He saved us through the washing of rebirth and renewal by the Holy Spirit, whom He poured out on us generously through Jesus Christ our Savior, so that, having been justified by His grace, we might become heirs having the hope of eternal life. (Titus 3:4–7)

Rather than helping people to be led to the truth, the lodge actually leads people away from it by teaching a falsehood contrary to the clear words of Scripture. In another of his letters St. Paul writes, "People will be lovers of themselves, ... having a form of godliness but denying its power. Have nothing to do with them" (2 Timothy 3:2, 5).

Another example of confused and false teaching with respect to God, humanity, and the immortality of the soul is this announcement from the Final Tribute to Deceased Members of the Fraternal Order of Eagles:

> It is not a final parting. The Fraternal Order of Eagles teaches that we shall meet again. Whether we look into the living eyes of those we love or gaze into the placid faces of our dead, love divine comforts us with the blessed assurance that this relation is eternal.

Or consider this statement from the Loyal Order of Moose burial service: "It is but parting; a journey to an unknown shore; a journey which we, too shall take—and at its end our Circle form again."

The Memorial Service of the Elks has this paragraph read by the Exalted Ruler:

> As Elks we are taught that some day the mortal shall put on immortality. Firm in our faith, we are reminded by these services that we are born, not to die, but to live. True, the light of beloved eyes has faded from our sight, but it shines more brightly upon another shore. Voices we loved to hear at the fireside, in marts of trade, or in fraternal association, are silenced; but they will live again in the music of the Choir Invisible and blend forever in the harmony of angels. Memorial Day with us is a day of tender sentiment. Hope dries our tears, and with eyes of faith we may see those whom we loved and lost awhile,

faring on through a better land, awaiting the day when the chain of fraternal love shall be reunited forevermore.

The preceding statements from burial and memorial services demonstrate that the various lodge organizations offer the assurance of an eternal reward. This assurance is given based not on the lodge member's faith in Jesus Christ, but on the basis of lodge membership and the member's wholesome life.

It should be clear from the foregoing that the theology of the lodge is well developed, an integral part of the member's, and completely false. It is the religion of well-meaning but misguided people. Their sincerity does not make it the truth.

4

Prayer in the Lodge

A s we demonstrated earlier, the lodge thinks of itself as being *above* any particular religion. Seeking to offend none, it mixes together portions of the belief-systems of many. This practice is called "syncretism." To many, the result seems quite "American," apart from any lodge connection, given our political view of tolerance. But political tolerance does not mean agreement in religious beliefs— which is what the lodge teaches.

Lodge prayers offer a clear example of syncretism, and lodge rites, ceremonies, and meetings always include prayer.

> In the opening of the lodge, the Great Architect of the Universe must be worshiped, and his blessings upon the work about to be done must be supplicated; at the same time, prayer should be offered for peace and harmony in the closing of the lodge. (Hertel's *Bible,* p. 34)

As with other portions of the lodge ritual mentioned previously (see chapter 3), lodge prayers intentionally shun of the name of Jesus. Yet the biblical teaching is that prayer is acceptable to God *only* when offered in the name of Jesus: "For there is one God and one mediator between God and men, the man Christ Jesus, who gave Himself as a ransom for all men" (1 Timothy 2:5–6). "I tell you the truth, My Father will give you whatever you ask in My name" (John 16:23).

The reason why Jesus Christ is omitted from lodge prayers is that the lodge attempts to be universal. "[I]ts universality is its boast. In its language citizens of every nation may converse; at its altars men of all religions may kneel; to its creed disciples of every faith may subscribe"

> **P**rayer to a deity is a fundamental dogma of Masonry. But who is this "Great Architect" that must be worshiped? Any god you design.

(*Encyclopedia of Freemasonry,* vol. 1, p. 149). Pike claims that at Masonic altars "the Christian, the Hebrew, the Moslem, the Brahmin, the followers of Confucius and Zoroaster, can assemble as brethren and unite in prayer to the one God." (*Morals and Dogma,* p. 226).

> The chaplain of the masonic lodge who prays as the voice of the lodge does not pray in the name of the Carpenter of Nazareth or the name of Jehovah or the name of Allah. He prays to the Grand Artificer or the Great Architect of the Universe. Under that title men of all faiths may find each his own deity. Failure to mention any deity by name *is not denial, but merely the practice of a gracious courtesy,* so that each man for whom prayer is offered can hear the name of his own deity in the all inclusive title of Great Architect. (*Short Talk Bulletin,* 36:8, p. 7; emphasis added)

Contrast the above writings of leading Masonic authors to the teaching of Jesus: "The Father ... has entrusted all judgment to the Son, that all may honor the Son just as they honor the Father. He who does not honor the Son does not honor the Father, who sent Him" (John 5:22–23).

Some Christians point out that a person can pray "in Jesus' name" yet not actually speak aloud the name. That being true, they point to (for example) the following two prayers and ask what might be wrong with them.

O Lord, we beseech Thee to bless the work of our Order. May the lessons we here teach be the means of making us better in Thy sight. May we practice in our daily lives the trustful faith of Job. (From the Ritual of the Order of Job's Daughters)

Go with this sister every step of this initiation, show her that we teach Thy truth, not only for this moment, but for life eternal. Amen. (Prayer prayed before the White Altar of Holy Promise of the Order of Rainbow)

In a Christian worship context, the above wording is fine. However, when such prayers are offered as part of rituals that do not permit the name of Christ as Savior and Redeemer, they are not Christian. Jesus said that to deny Him before men would bring His denial of us before His Father in heaven (Matthew 10:33).

Are we saying, then, that the prayers of the lodge are not true prayer? On the other hand, is God forced to listen to us just because we happened to use the form of prayer? In order to answer, think through what prayer is.

Consider this statement: Prayer is conversing with the Triune God, in whom we live and who lives in us. As Jesus said, "Your Father knows what you need before you ask Him" (Matthew 6:8). The Lord we have always intimately involves Himself in our lives—in our thoughts, our goals, our actions, our speech. Like an attentive father who watches over his children, so the heavenly Father watches over us, His children by faith in Jesus. The relationship is very intimate. Therefore, we cannot tell Him anything He does not already know.

What is the motivating power in our prayers? Is it not the Holy Spirit who lives in us, that is, in our bodies, which are His temples? Christian prayer is the Holy Spirit putting us on the same frequency as God, as in a radio transmission. Prayer presupposes the relationship of the individual with the Father. This relationship was created when the Holy Spirit worked saving faith in the heart of the individual, who now believes that Jesus Christ died to pay for all his or her sins and rose again to defeat death, the devil, and the powers of evil all around. Prayer is the *result* of conversion, after which communication with God—prayer—is possible. Thus, only Christians can pray legitimate prayers heard by the Father, because prayer and everything else in the Christian's life—as a Christian—is done under the grace of God in the name and to the glory of Jesus Christ, the God made flesh! This is not what the lodge teaches. The lodge ritual intentionally avoids Christ in its prayers. Therefore, such prayers cannot be considered valid.

Every Christian needs the conviction of the girl who was asked to pray a public prayer at which many non-Christians would be present. The daughter of a Baptist minister, she wrote her prayer and ended it with the phrase "in Jesus' name." When she showed her prayer to the vice-principal of the school, he suggested that she revise it by omitting that phrase because "we wanted a nondenominational prayer that would satisfy everyone." He suggested saying, "in God's name." The girl refused. A prayer without the phrase tacked on might have been permissible if all the people were Christian. But in this case, it was to avoid being identified with Christ. Thus, it denied Him.

The Christian should be able to sing everywhere:

> All hail the power of Jesus' name!
> Let angels prostrate fall;
> Bring forth the royal diadem
> And crown Him Lord of all.

5

Some Doctrinal Comparisons

E very Christian should have great concern for preserving his or her biblical heritage lest it be lost through neglect and/or accommodation.

Through Moses, God told the Israelites to make every home a school with the parents responsible for continually telling their children about their heritage as God's chosen people and the great acts performed in their behalf by a gracious God (Deuteronomy 6:6–25). Joshua, too, at the settlement of the Promised Land, warned the people never to forsake the Lord's ways (Joshua 24). Jesus exhorted His followers to remain in His teaching (John 8:31–32; 15:7). St. Paul warned Timothy about people who would try to remove the truth from Christianity, which he preached, a warning he strongly gave during his final imprisonment in Rome (1 and 2 Timothy). It was a warning he also gave to the pastors of Asia Minor at his tear-filled Miletus farewell (Acts 20:29–31). St. John repeatedly warned his "little children" about those who would corrupt the teachings of the Redeemer (1 John 2:18–26; 3:7).

The Bible is full of admonishment and warning not to let the teaching of Scripture be lost. In this spirit these words are written as a warning. Our neglect of, ignorance of, or refusal to evaluate what the lodge cult teaches is to invite its influence upon our lives. Just as eternal vigilance is the price Americans must pay to keep their political freedoms from being removed, so also must we do the same with our spiritual heritage. Therefore, we review some of the major differences between the religion of the lodge and Christianity.

The Lodge Does Not Understand Christianity

Based on the quotations from leading Masonic writers, they have not understood Christianity properly. The quotations portray Christianity as a morally upright life, with eternal life as its reward. In that picture, the Creator is a benevolent God who, with great tolerance, overlooks our many excusable imperfections and who approvingly ushers us into the great beyond. The lodge teachings are nothing but works-righteousness cloaked in flowery language, holding out eternal hope to the faithful.

> There are only two religions in all the world. The man-centered religion of salvation by works says, "You do it, and God will bless you." The God-centered religion of salvation through faith says, "It has all been done for you; accept it in faith as a free gift given to you."

What a sham! In America, where the Christian religion is still the dominant religion practiced, lodge organizations have made Christianity something it is not: a system of moral values that can be kept quite decently by even those who are not Christians. Thus, the lodge brings in even those excluded by the church and thinks by so doing they are more in harmony with the truth. The lodge, therefore, is not only of the opinion that it is above Christianity but also an improvement on it.

Comparing Theologies of God

The Masonic Lodge regards as essential the belief in a

supreme being—so strongly that they ousted an entire atheistic congregation from their premises. An atheistic Rabbi and his 140 member congregation in Birmingham, MI, were refused further use of the Masonic Temple in early 1965. The *St. Louis Post-Dispatch,* March 21, 1965, said that "theological reasons" were given as the basis for the decision. The lodge insisted that a positive commitment to the existence of some kind of supreme being was required for use of their temple.

> We have but one dogma, a belief in God, but this is so firmly established as the principal foundation stone of the brotherhood that no one can ever be admitted a member of an English speaking lodge without a full and free acceptance thereof. In all reference to the Deity, God is reverently spoken of as the Great Architect of the Universe. ... Upon this foundation stone we construct a simple religious faith—the Fatherhood of God, the Brotherhood of Man, and the Immortality of the Soul—simple, but all-efficient. By reason of this simple creed, Freemasonry has been able to attract and accept as members of the Fraternity adherents of every religious faith in the world—Christians, Jews, Hindus, Mohammendans, Pharisees, Buddhists, and others—atheists alone being excluded. ("Freemasonry—A Simple Religious Faith," *Royal Arch Mason,* V:9, March 1957)

Although the lodge demands belief in a supreme being and uses words like *Lord, God,* and others, it very carefully avoids a confession of the God of Scripture. The lodge refuses even to define God. It goes no farther than to give Him a name, the most common being the Great or Grand Architect of the Universe. Carl Claudy, in *Introduc-*

tion to Freemasonry (2:110), writes, "[The Mason] must declare his faith in a Supreme Being before he may be initiated. But note that he is not required to say, then or ever, what God. He may name Him as he will, think of Him as he pleases; make Him impersonal law or personal and anthropomorphic; Freemasonry cares not" (Quoted in *Secret Teachings,* p. 111).

To say that the only true God is the Triune God would be offensive to the lodge, because that is too narrow of an understanding for purposes of the lodge. The Father, the Son, and the Holy Spirit is the Christian's God, three persons yet one God. This the lodge rejects as being sectarian.

It really becomes an offense to the lodge when the name of Jesus comes up. The Christian believes that the Word became flesh and lived among us (John 1:14) in the person of Jesus of Nazareth. Therefore, Jesus is true God and true man, divine and human. The Son of God became a human being in order to die as the payment for the sins of the world. Jesus became like the lambs slain during Old Testament times to carry away the sins of the people. Jesus is the "Lamb of God, who takes away the sin of the world" (John 1:29). Jesus makes it quite clear that He alone is the only way to eternal life with God: "I am the way and the truth and the life. No one comes to the Father except through Me" (John 14:6). Tell the lodge to confess that and see what happens!

> The "animal lodges" generally do not use substitute names for God. They simply expect candidates for membership to affirm their belief in God. The major problem for Christianity is still their veiled teaching of salvation by works or personal goodness.

In the experience of this writer, most Christians who are members of the lodge do not share our concern over the Masonic compromise of God. They have been duped. Most often these members had no idea of what they were getting into before they took "the pledge." Others feel that the business and social advantages are more important than standing up for Jesus. So it becomes easier for them to say that they see nothing wrong with using a different name for God inasmuch as for them it is the Triune God that they worship in the lodge.

Comparing Theologies of Humanity

The lodge does not say that humanity has a problem with *sin*. Masonry teaches its adherents that the candidate coming into the lodge has a "rough and imperfect nature." That is why Masonry uses the Ashlar, Gavel, Square, and Compass—to remind the members that they ever must work out their imperfections in order to be found acceptable to the "Supreme Grand Master" and to achieve a life in paradise, the "Grand Lodge Above." Simple! Now there is no need for a Savior—so the lodge teaches.

Thousands have bought into this lie. Jesus taught otherwise. "I am the resurrection and the life. He who *believes in Me* will live, even though he dies; and whoever lives and *believes in Me* will never die" (John 11:25–26; emphasis added).

The discussion that many committed Christians have had for years with various lodge organizations parallels the discussion Jesus had with the Jews of His day as recorded in John 8:12–59. These religious leaders and teachers of the day were highly regarded by the people. Yet they could not accept the teaching that Jesus was the light of the world, the only hope of salvation. Instead, they clung to the idea that some personal qualification (being a descendant of Abraham) guaranteed them a place in heaven. Jesus had to tell them that their father was not Abraham, as they thought, but the devil: "He was a murderer from the beginning, not holding to the truth, for there is no truth in him. When he lies, he speaks his native language, for he is a liar and the father of lies" (John 8:44).

So also today lodge members are taught the lie that lodge teachings provide the light necessary to illuminate the darkness in which they are walking. They are also taught the lie that right shaping of personal character will guarantee a place in heaven.

People are *sinners,* not merely "good" along with a few imperfections. St. Paul had to confess, "I know that nothing good lives in me, that is, in my sinful nature" (Romans 7:18). The psalmist admits: "Surely I was sinful at birth, sinful from the time my mother conceived me" (Psalm 51:5). And he begs God, "Wash away all my iniquity and cleanse me from my sin. For I know my transgressions, and my sin is always before me. Against You, You only, have I sinned and done what is evil in Your sight" (Psalm 51:2–4).

Would lodge members in their rituals say these things? Is this what the lodge teaches? No! Such talk would be forbidden. The lodge considers humanity to be "above" such wretchedness.

Comparing Theologies on Reaching Heaven

Some of what has been said already has made this comparison, so we will not repeat it all. We need to keep clear, however, the teachings of the lodge: that people earn their heavenly home by squaring their actions and ordering their paths according to the moral principals inculcated in lodge teaching. Instead of emphasizing that having eternal life is by God's grace alone, through Christ Jesus alone, the lodge lays it out as the reward for becoming a member of the Order.

Although the lodge assumes we should have no problem accepting its teaching about the afterlife because the belief is so common, Christianity is the only religion knowing that eternal life is a free gift of God. Heaven cannot be earned. No amount of good works, charitable deeds, clean living, great moral values, etc., will accord a person a home in heaven. Such a home is a gift. One cannot earn a gift. If it is earned, it no longer is a gift.

How comforting to know and believe the promise of the Messiah! "Do not let your hearts be troubled. Trust in God; trust also in Me. In My Father's house are many rooms; if it were not so, I would have told you. I am going there to prepare a place for you. And if I go and prepare a place for you, I will come back and take you to be with Me that you also may be where I am" (John 14:1–3).

Comparing Theologies concerning the "Sacred Volume"

Another conflict deals with what role the Bible plays in the life of the lodge. The Bible is considered a sacred volume, but just one of many. True, the lodge requires the presence of a "Sacred Volume" as one of the three indispensable "great lights" of the lodge temple. However, that "Sacred Volume" can be whatever the lodge wants it to be. The book used will be determined by the religious beliefs of the majority of the members of that lodge. It could be the Torah, the Qur'an, the Veda, etc.

But even if the book chosen is the Bible, remember that it is only on display. It is not used as Christians use the Bible. The lodge, which has developed its own educational system, cannot regard the Holy Scriptures as the only inspired, infallible, inerrant Word of God. It cannot, because its sectarian membership forbids it, as does the theology of the lodge.

Comparing Theologies
concerning Prayer

Enough lodge prayers have already been quoted, in whole or in part, upon which to make judgments. Whereas the lodge prayer strives not to offend any of those praying, it really ends up giving super offense to the Christian—and, I suspect, to other religions as well. The avoidance of the scripturally revealed name of God does not allow a prayer to be palatable for the Christian. The Christian, knowing that the Lord Jesus leads the believer in his or her daily walk through life, would never tolerate the wishy-washy prayer to the "Nameless One of a Hundred Names." We Christians, praying in the name of Jesus, always address the Triune God.

The Christian prayer life is very personal, because it reaches to the depths of our souls. We share it cautiously and selectively. When someone else prays with us, speaking the words in our behalf (as in a worship service), we have given them permission to talk to God for us. It is neither safe nor right to permit others to lead us in prayer unless we trust their beliefs. Neither a Jewish Worshipful Master or a Unitarian Masonic Chaplain accepts the Triune God or Jesus as true God and man. It follows, then, that it is unthinkable for a Christian Mason to permit them to lead him in prayer. This is so obvious that one wonders how any Christian can accept such a situation.

A Final Thought

Some lodge members say that the lodge's use of the name of God is no different from including His name in the American pledge of allegiance or saying "So help me God" in a court room oath. The difference, however, is huge.

The civic use of the word *God* does not define Him or

teach that everyone's understanding of God has equal validity *in eternity*. The state's concern is only that, whatever a person's belief, he or she live according to that belief.

Even the purpose of living according to one's own belief in the civic arena differs greatly from the purpose that the lodge has in mind. The state desires a moral life simply for the sake of the prosperity of the state; the lodge teaches morality for the sake of earning eternal life. Nor does the state try to explain why people's behavior is not always moral (nor, obviously, whether the "why" has any impact on eternal life). Here again, the lodge has an answer: humanity is basically good but with minor imperfections—and, therefore, by implication has an inherent claim on eternal life.

In conclusion, the state's use of the term *God* is for civic peace only. The lodge, however, involves itself as a religion for the sake of the member's eternal welfare—with a message contrary to that of Jesus Christ. Our goal as Christians is to witness to that difference, not to attack others, but to clearly testify to what God has done for us through His Son.

Continued membership in the lodge gives support not only to the good the lodge does but also to its false teachings—which can and do lead innocent souls into hell. Souls are perishing for an eternity because people have chosen to follow the way of the lodge. Tragic!

6

Oaths and Secrecy in the Lodge

The issues of the lodge's oaths and secrecy do not fall into the same category as its doctrinal teachings about humanity, sin, God, salvation, and achieving eternal life. Occasions within the church and society may require an oath or some secrecy, and one's faith need not be compromised. However, the Christian needs to evaluate what is being sworn to and what the secret is in order to determine whether to take the oath or keep the secret.

Lodge Oaths

The lodge asks its members to take an oath every step of the way. Supposedly, they take these oaths seriously. Consider, though, the conflict that creates for Christians and/or governmental officials who pledge contradictory oaths.

For example, evaluate the lodge oath to support a fellow member. The Royal Arch Degree requires the candidate to swear, "I will assist a Companion Royal Arch Mason when I see him engaged in any difficulty, and will espouse his cause so far as to extricate him from the same, whether he be right or wrong" (*Duncan's Masonic Ritual and Monitor,* p. 230). Defend and give aid to fellow lodge members even when they are wrong or have broken the law? Can you imagine a defendant, a lawyer, a judge, and a member of a jury, all being Royal Arch Masons, bringing justice to bear in a case? (The Blue Lodge, however, does except murder and treason.)

The oath to support fellow lodge members is expressed often by showing favoritism in employment, letting of contracts, business deals, and other functions of society. Discrimination in favor of lodge members is practiced all the time, every day. As citizens, Christians ought to make business decisions on better criteria than mere membership in the same club.

Another lodge oath requires members to always conceal and never reveal what goes on in the lodge. The problem comes not so much with the oath but that those who terminate membership in the lodge often receive recriminations in their job, station in life, position in a company, etc. This writer has sat with many who have suffered this way. Some were not intimidated by the lodge and made a clean break. Many others, however, were and are intimidated from completely removing ("demitting") themselves from lodge membership. So they stay, trying to minimize the influence the lodge has in their life. The result is a compromise of their innermost thoughts, principles, and integrity. People around them can see the "games" they play.

> Why does Masonry stress the importance of secrecy? (1) The element of secrecy attracts men and makes them feel important. (2) Secrecy provides a stabilizing influence—something important enough to be secret must be defended at all costs. (3) By means of secrecy, Masonry can hide its religious nature and secure converts who would not otherwise join. (*Secret Teachings,* pp. 30–31)

Secrecy in the Lodge

We call attention to the secrecy of the lodge, not because we think it is a major offense or that we are jealous of lodge secrets. Rather, we are concerned for the effects secrecy has on the individual lodge member in his relationship with those around him—his family, his church, his neighbors. (In any case, most lodges, including the Masonic, have been demonstrably unsuccessful in maintaining secrecy. We even know the most high secret names of the Grand Architect of the Universe, *Mah—Ha—Bone* and *Jah—Bul—On*.)

The prescribed secrecy prohibits the member from sharing his lodge life with anyone, even his own wife. This breaks his wedding vows. Then, if he is a member of a Christian congregation, he will not talk about his lodge life with his pastor, erecting a wall between them. This writer has on many occasions discussed lodge teachings, actions, and membership with many Masons. For the most part it is a monolog. When that happens, the pastor-parishioner relationship deteriorates, and the brotherhood built around the blood of Christ dissolves due to some secret oath that even most lodge members consider a bit silly.

Many people do not realize that the secrecy allows for all sorts of discrimination—for example, against those who have a physical defect like a missing finger, an amputated limb, one eye, etc., as well as against those who are of the wrong nationality/race, the wrong social standing, or the wrong anything else. A single member may drop the "black ball" of rejection into the box, thereby ending any possibility of a candidate being accepted.

If what the lodge has to offer is so good, so righteous, so admirable, so important even for eternal life, then why the veil of secrecy? The whole world ought to be invited in, for to exclude any would be to exclude them from eternal life in heaven (the "Grand Lodge Above"). Instead, the doors are open only to some.

An oath changes a general commitment into a binding agreement, with God as witness and judge. Therefore, one ought never take an oath without prior prayer and thought. Yet lodge candidates are called on to take the oath of secrecy even before they know what it is they must keep secret upon great pain. Some lodge members have claimed that they took the oath merely as a formality. Such an attitude is dishonesty toward the lodge itself, as well as before the Lord, who witnessed the oath. Christians should expect better of themselves.

In the matter of oaths and secrecy, Christians need to remember their very special status before the living Lord. "Don't you know that you yourselves are God's temple and that God's Spirit lives in you? If anyone destroys God's temple, God will destroy him; for God's temple is sacred, and you are that temple" (1 Corinthians 3:16–17). "Do you not know that your body is a temple of the Holy Spirit, who is in you, whom you have received from God? *You are not your own; you were bought with a price.* Therefore honor God with your body" (1 Corinthians 6:19–20, emphasis added).

7

How to Witness to the Lodge Member

Education concerning the differences between the lodge and Christianity began in my denomination, The Lutheran Church—Missouri Synod, in 1849. For nearly 150 years our church has been a leader among the nation's denominations in providing factual information about those teachings and practices of the lodge that conflict with the Bible. This small book, a revision of an earlier volume, continues that educational process, making available to individuals and/or groups information for and encouragement to "always be prepared to give an answer to everyone who asks you to give the reason for the hope that you have" (1 Peter 3:15).

Convincing lodge members and candidates to "come out and be separate" from the lodge is possible; many people have done so. The task, however, can be difficult. Therefore, here are some tips to keep in mind when talking with a lodge member.

First, secrecy will keep in-depth discussions from happening. It is a barrier that one must accept. Only the Holy Spirit can overcome this wall. Depend on Him to work through you and your words. He will!

Second, when people are instructed into the lodge, they often are unable to recognize that lodge teachings contradict Christian teachings because they know too little of Christianity. At the same time, the meaning of the lodge (as, for example, symbolized by the Lambskin Apron) seems so pure and simple. The person may contend that the lodge in no way interferes with his church life; in fact, he may claim that it helps it. This attitude usually means that the door is closed to any further discussion. Don't try to beat down the door; pray for the Lord to do it.

> **A**t that time you will be given what to say, for it will not be you speaking, but the Spirit of your Father speaking through you. (Matthew 10:19–20)

Third, after taking the oath, paying the dues, and enjoying the fraternal atmosphere, the person will not be likely to admit to an error in judgment. To do so would take genuine repentance and humility—and human nature is not inclined to either. Most people become defensive instead.

Four, the pressure applied by fellow lodge members is often intense. The consequences of leaving the lodge may be life long.

Careful planning and thought needs to precede our witness to a lodge member. We need to "take it to the Lord in prayer." We should be specific in such prayers, remembering the person by name, and asking the Lord for a specific action. At the same time, avoid the more common mistakes when witnessing to a lodge member:

- Don't make statements that are not true or not factual.
- Don't say things in such a stern, dogmatic way that it tends to end discussion.
- Don't begin with the statement "My church says it is wrong to join the lodge."
- Don't argue to the point of anger or with a raised voice of impatience.

These mistakes will lose the argument every time with

every person.

Knowledge about what the lodge teaches and practices is most important in witnessing to the lodge member or candidate. Leaving some reading material about the lodge-Christian conflict may be helpful (if delivered with understanding, humility, and patience), but the lodge member may accept it only to get rid of you. Personal sharing generally accomplishes more.

Knowing what the actual conflicts are between the lodge and Christianity will arm you with confidence and certainty, necessary if the discussion tends to become heated. More important is this: When you really know the facts and really love the person—really know and really love—then you can ask penetrating and thought-provoking questions in a humble, contrite spirit that will be nonthreatening to the lodge member.

It is not too difficult to help a lodge member see his own contradictions if the right questions are asked. The following is one example of how the question approach can work:

Question: It is my understanding that the lodge prides itself in its educational program.

Answer: Yes, we do require our members to know a few things.

Question: Would you share a little with me?

Answer: Well, I can't tell you much, but if you care to join, you would learn it all.

Question: Is what you learn in the lodge important to you?

Answer: Yes.

Question: Well, then, it should be important to me also. Why must I join first in order to learn something that will help me? Why shouldn't everyone be told?

(It is not important to carry this question on any further because the point is obvious. Move on.)

Question: Is the lodge a religion to you?

Answer: Absolutely not!

Question: Do you pray in the lodge?

Answer: Yes, but it's only to open our meetings.

Question: Do you pray to God?

Answer: Of course we do.

Question: Who does the lodge say God is?

Answer: We don't tell any member who God is; each person if free to think of God as he wants.

Question: Is that what the Bible teaches?

Answer: Not all members believe the way Christians do.

Question: If you were leading the lodge in prayer, could you use the name of the Triune God, ending the prayer with "This we pray in Jesus' name"?

Answer: We use the prayers printed in our book.

(Now the person will realize that someone else has predetermined what the prayers are to be; that the Bible is rejected by some "lodge brothers"; and that avoidance of the Triune God is really a denial of Him—all of which will result in leaving a "crack" in the fraternal relationship he has. Doubt will begin.)

Obviously, the conversation needs to continue, but this short example gives you an idea of both the style and content of the question approach. Remember, though: questions need to be asked without sarcasm, in complete humility and understanding, yet firmly headed toward the goal of demonstrating the conflict existing between the lodge and Christianity. Remember also that unless the lodge member is convinced in his own heart that he is wrong, he is still going to retain the same opinion. As someone has said, "A man convinced against his will is of the same opinion still."

The ultimate goal, that of changing a lodge member to a former lodge member, is achieved only by the working of the Holy Spirit; He alone can change people's hearts. He does this when we use words that point to our sins and our forgiveness in Jesus. Nowhere else will people hear the Good News of salvation, of the redeeming work of Christ, other than from a Christian source. Even if the lodge member claims to be a Christian, he still needs to hear the message of salvation from us. Simple words, not sermons, about the cross of Jesus are the most important words anyone could hear—professing Christians included!

We all need love and acceptance and look forward to receiving it from one another. Jesus loves us, even though we have sinned. We, too, need to love one another, even when we all have sinned. If we can and do, then long-lasting relationships will result based on the blood of Christ, our Savior from all sin. This will deeply impress lodge members, especially those who are watching one of their own dissociate himself from them, and may be just the factor keeping any recriminations from happening as a result of becoming an ex-lodge member.

May the Lord Jesus bless your efforts!

Conclusion

The objections a Christian has with regard to certain organizations may be summarized as follows:

1. They claim to offer moral and spiritual enlightenment that is not available in Holy Scripture.
2. They teach that all religions ultimately worship the same God but under different names.
3. They declare that all people have equal access to God, their attitude toward Jesus Christ being unimportant.
4. They teach that eternal life is the reward that God gives for virtuous living.

False teachings and practices always destroy the freedom that the Gospel of Christ gives. Falsehoods are shackles that chain us in the darkness of unbelief. No conflict between the lodge and Christianity would exist if the lodge did not seriously believe and teach a way of salvation. However, lodge members do—and they are just as serious about their lodge heritage as we are about our Christian heritage; we want it preserved among us. It won't be if we allow the teachings of the lodge to be accepted by our people. But then, neither can the lodge exist if the truth of Christianity prevails among us. Onward Christian soldiers! Stand up for Jesus!

Resources

Ankerberg, John, and John Weldon. *The Secret Teachings of the Masonic Lodge: A Christian Perspective.* Chicago: Moody Press, 1989.

Duncan, Malcolm C. *Duncan's Masonic Ritual and Monitor* (Revised Edition). Chicago: Ezra A. Cook Publications, 1960.

Morey, Robert. *The Truth about Masons.* Eugene, OR: Harvest House Publishers, 1993.

Pike, Albert. *Morals and Dogma.* 1871. Reprinted at Richmond, VA: L. H. Jenkins, Inc., 1928.

Whalen, William J. *Christianity and American Freemasonry* (Revised Edition). Huntington, IN: Our Sunday Visitor Publishing, 1987.

Various releases on specific lodges are available from the Commission on Organizations of The Lutheran Church—Missouri Synod, 1333 S. Kirkwood Road, St. Louis, MO 63122-7295.